The Rainforest
Grew All Around

By Susan K. Mitchell   Illustrated by Connie McLennan

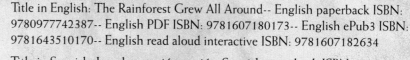

To Joseph, for whom my love grows infinitely—SKM
To Thomas: survivor, hero—CKM

Thanks to David Oren of the Nature Conservancy,
Amazon Conservation Program for verifying the accuracy
of the information in this book.

Title in English: The Rainforest Grew All Around-- English paperback ISBN: 9780977742387-- English PDF ISBN: 9781607180173-- English ePub3 ISBN: 9781643510170-- English read aloud interactive ISBN: 9781607182634

Title in Spanish: La selva creció y creió-- Spanish paperback ISBN: 9781628553697-- Spanish PDF ISBN: 9781934359525-- Spanish ePub3 ISBN: 9781643511757-- Spanish read aloud interactive ISBN: 9781628550948

Portuguese Title: A Floresta Tropical se Espalhou por Toda Parte-- Portuguese paperback ISBN: 9781643513270-- Portuguese PDF ISBN: 9781643513287-- Portuguese ePub3 ISBN: 9781643513294-- Portuguese read aloud interactive ISBN: 9781643513300

French Title: La forêt tropicale pousse à la verticale-- French paperback ISBN: 9781643516219-- French read aloud interactive ISBN: 9781643516240

Chinese Title: 雨林，生机处处 --Chinese paperback ISBN: 9781607183921-- Chinese PDF ISBN: 9781607183983 --Chinese ePub3 ISBN: 9781643515304-- Chinese read aloud interactive ISBN: 9781628551990

Arabic Title: الغابة المطيرة نمت في كل مكان-- Arabic paperback ISBN: 9781643514499-- Arabic PDF ISBN: 9781643514505-- Arabic ePub3 ISBN: 9781643514512-- Arabic read aloud interactive ISBN: 9781643514529

Indonesian Title: Hutan Hujan Tumbuh di Sekelilingnya-- Indonesian paperback ISBN: 9781643513898-- Indonesian PDF ISBN: 9781643513904-- Indonesian ePub3 ISBN: 9781643513911-- Indonesian read aloud interactive ISBN: 9781643513928

Printed in the US
This product conforms to CPSIA 2008

Arbordale Publishing
formerly Sylvan Dell Publishing
Mt. Pleasant, SC
www.ArbordalePublishing.com

ON THE GROUND,
there fell a seed . . .
the fluffiest seed
that you ever did see.

The seed in the ground,

and the rainforest grew
all around, all around;
the rainforest grew all around.

Between seventy and one hundred inches of rain fall in the Amazon Rainforest each year.

The Amazon River is over 4,000 miles long and rises over 40 feet during the rainy season just because of the rain.

A rainforest receives an average of at least 60 inches of rain per year.

Kapok trees can grow between 150 and 200 feet—as tall as a 15 to 20-story building!

Kapoks, also called Ceiba or Silk Cotton trees, grow in Africa, and Central and South America.

AND FROM THE SEED,
there grew a tree . . .
the tallest tree
that you ever did see.

The tree from the seed,
and the seed in the ground,

and the rainforest grew
all around, all around;
the rainforest grew all around.

Jaguars' spots help them to hide in the rainforest shadows.

They spend their days dozing on tree branches and their nights hunting.

AND IN THE TREE,
there lay a cat . . .
the spottiest cat
that you ever did see.

The cat in the tree,
and the tree from the seed,
and the seed in the ground,

and the rainforest grew
all around, all around;
the rainforest grew all around.

Vines wrap around and climb the trees looking for sunlight.

Thick, woody vines called lianas are usually as thick as an adult's arm.

AND NEAR THE CAT,

there was a vine . . .
the curliest vine
that you ever did see.

The vine near the cat,
and the cat in the tree,
and the tree from the seed,
and the seed in the ground,

and the rainforest grew
all around, all around;
the rainforest grew all around.

ᴀɴᴅ ʙʏ ᴛʜᴇ ᴠɪɴᴇ,
there was a snake . . .
the greenest snake
that you ever did see.

The snake by the vine,
and the vine near the cat,
and the cat in the tree,
and the tree from the seed,
and the seed in the ground,

and the rainforest grew
all around, all around;
the rainforest grew all around.

Emerald tree boas curl up
in the vines and live high in
the trees.

They have really long teeth
to help them catch and
hold their prey.

Leafcutter ants climb high into the trees and clip off leaves.

Ants pick up and carry the leaves to a kind of "garden" in their underground nest.

They eat the fungi that grow on the dead leaves.

And by the snake, there crawled an ant . . . the busiest ant that you ever did see.

The ant by the snake, and the snake by the vine, and the vine near the cat, and the cat in the tree, and the tree from the seed, and the seed in the ground,

and the rainforest grew all around, all around; the rainforest grew all around.

A ND NEAR THE ANT,
there was a sloth . . .
the slowest sloth
that you ever did see.

The sloth near the ant,
and the ant by the snake,
and the snake by the vine,
and the vine near the cat,
and the cat in the tree,
and the tree from the seed,
and the seed in the ground,

and the rainforest grew
all around, all around;
the rainforest grew all around.

Sloths hang upside-down in the trees and move very slowly.

Sloth moths live in sloth fur. When sloths climb down the tree to go to the bathroom, the moths jump out, lay eggs in the droppings, and then jump back into the fur for the ride back up the tree.

Bromeliads can grow on other plants but do not hurt the "parent" plants.

Most have round clusters of leaves that catch rain and make "little ponds."

AND BY THE SLOTH,
there was a plant . . .
the prettiest plant
that you ever did see.

The plant by the sloth,
and the sloth near the ant,
and the ant by the snake,
and the snake by the vine,
and the vine near the cat,
and the cat in the tree,
and the tree from the seed,
and the seed in the ground,

and the rainforest grew
all around, all around;
the rainforest grew all around.

Pineapples are bromeliads
that grow in the ground.

Female poison dart frogs lay their eggs in a safe place to hatch: under a leaf.

After hatching, the males carry the tadpoles to separate bromeliad ponds so each one will have enough to eat.

If something happens to one tadpole, another tadpole may be safe in a different bromeliad pond.

AND IN THE PLANT,
there was a frog . . .
the brightest frog
that you ever did see.

The frog in the plant,
and the plant by the sloth,
and the sloth near the ant,
and the ant by the snake,
and the snake by the vine,
and the vine near the cat,
and the cat in the tree,
and the tree from the seed,
and the seed in the ground,

and the rainforest grew
all around, all around;
the rainforest grew all around.

Toucans use their large beaks to pluck fruit from trees.

They also eat bugs, small lizards, and the eggs and chicks of other birds.

A ND BY THE FROG,
there sat a bird . . .
the funniest bird
that you ever did see.

The bird by the frog,
and the frog in the plant,
and the plant by the sloth,
and the sloth near the ant,
and the ant by the snake,
and the snake by the vine,
and the vine near the cat,
and the cat in the tree,
and the tree from the seed,
and the seed in the ground,

and the rainforest grew
all around, all around;
the rainforest grew all around.

Fruit and nectar-feeding bats are important to the survival of the rainforest because they help to pollinate flowers and spread seeds of trees and plants.

Fruit bats find the fruit and flowers by sight, smell, and echolocation—they send out very high-pitched noises and listen to the sounds bouncing back. They know where things are by the sounds.

AND NEAR THE BIRD,
there hung a bat . . .
the sleepiest bat
that you ever did see.

The bat near the bird,
and the bird by the frog,
and the frog in the plant,
and the plant by the sloth,
and the sloth near the ant,
and the ant by the snake,
and the snake by the vine,
and the vine near the cat,
and the cat in the tree,
and the tree from the seed,
and the seed in the ground,

and the rainforest grew
all around, all around;
the rainforest grew all around.

Bats are the only mammals that fly. Just like other mammals, they have hair (not feathers).

Their wings are their "hands" and have digits, just like our fingers—including the thumb!

AND BY THE BAT,
there was a pod . . .
the highest pod
that you ever did see.

 The pod by the bat,
 and the bat near the bird,
 and the bird by the frog,
 and the frog in the plant,
 and the plant by the sloth,
 and the sloth near the ant,
 and the ant by the snake,
 and the snake by the vine,
 and the vine near the cat,
 and the cat in the tree,
 and the tree from the seed,
 and the seed in the ground,

and the rainforest grew
all around, all around;
the rainforest grew all around.

The flowers on the Kapok tree turn into large, hard pods that burst open.

Tiny little seeds inside the pods are covered with white fluff, called kapok.

The wind blows the kapok fluff and the seeds off to make new trees.

A ND FROM THE POD,
there blew a seed . . .
the fluffiest seed
that you ever did see.

The seed from the pod,
and the pod by the bat,
and the bat near the bird,
and the bird by the frog,
and the frog in the plant,
and the plant by the sloth,
and the sloth near the ant,
and the ant by the snake,
and the snake by the vine,
and the vine near the cat,
and the cat in the tree,
and the tree from the seed,
and the seed in the ground,
and the rainforest grew
all around, all around,
the rainforest grew all around.

For Creative Minds

Animal Adaptations

Adaptations help animals to live in their habitat: to get food and water, to protect themselves from predators, to survive weather, and even to help them make their homes. *Can you match the animals to the adaptations that help them live in the rainforest? Answers are upside-down at bottom of page.*

1. Their spots help them hide.
2. These mammals have wings to fly.
3. Their green coloring helps them to hide in the leaves.
4. Curved claws help them hold onto tree branches.
5. Bright colors warn other animals of their poison.
6. Large beaks and flexible necks help them pick fruit from the trees.
7. Fake eyes confuse would-be predators.
8. They use their strong jaws to cut leaves.

A. Sloths

B. Emerald Tree Boas

C. Toucans

D. Owl Butterflies

E. Bats

F. Leafcutter Ants

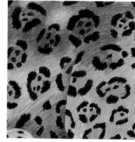
G. Jaguars

H. Poison Dart Frogs

1-G, 2-E, 3-B, 4-A, 5-H, 6-C, 7-D, 8-F

Seed Dispersal

Just like animals, plants have adaptations to help them survive in the rainforest and even in your own backyard. If seeds were to fall directly under the parent plant, the seedlings would not have enough room, sunlight, water, or nutrients to survive. Because of this, seeds get carried away from the parent in several different ways: *Can you match the seed or carrier to how the seeds are spread?*

1. Wind helps to blow seeds away from the parent. *Have you ever blown on dandelion thistles to make them "fly?"*

2. Animals eat the fruit or seeds. When the animals defecate (go to the bathroom), they leave the seeds far away from the parent plant.

3. Some seeds stick to the fur or hair of an animal. *Have you ever had anything stick to you or your clothes?*

4. Animals may bury seeds to eat later but then forget about them.

5. Humans plant seeds on purpose. *How do you think early humans first thought to plant seeds? How did it change their lives?*

6. Animals spread pollen from one plant to another when they fly.

7. Some seeds float on water.

A. Bumble bee on flower

E. Cocklebur on shoelace

B. Coconut in ocean

F. Squirrel with acorn

C. Corn in field

G. Maple "Whirlybirds"

D. Toucan eating fig

What Do We Use From the Rainforest?

Even though we may live a long way from a rainforest, we eat and use lots of things from the area. Air; medicines; mahogany and teak wood; rubber; chocolate; gum; Brazil nuts; cashews; coffee; coconuts; spices like pepper, cinnamon, and vanilla; and fruit like pineapples, bananas, mangos, and papayas are just some of the rainforest items that we use on a regular basis. *What are some items that we use just as they grow or come from the rainforest? What are some things that we use part of or change to make useful to us? What would happen if the rainforests were to disappear?*

Rainforest Cookies

These cookies use several ingredients that come from the rainforest.

Preheat oven to 375° F.

2 to 2 ¼ cups all purpose flour	½ cup brown **sugar**
1 tsp. baking soda	1 tsp. **vanilla** extract
1 tsp. salt	2 eggs
1 tsp. **cinnamon**	¼ cup sweetened **coconut** flakes
1 stick butter (1/2 cup), softened	4 cups (12 oz) **chocolate** chips
1 medium ripe **banana**	1 cup chopped **cashews**
½ cup granulated **sugar**	

Combine 2 cups flour, baking soda, salt, and cinnamon and set aside.

Beat butter, banana, and sugars until creamy.

Beat in eggs and then add the coconut flakes.

Gradually add flour mixture using extra flour if needed.

Stir in the chocolate chips and cashews.

Drop by rounded tablespoon onto an ungreased baking sheet.

Bake 10 to 12 minutes until golden brown.